LET'S LEARN ABOUT LITERATURE

POEMS

Heather
Moore Niver

Enslow Publishing
101 W. 23rd Street
Suite 240
New York, NY 10011
USA

enslow.com

WORDS TO KNOW

figure of speech A word or phrase that doesn't have its usual meaning.

literature Written work.

metaphor A word or phrase that compares two different things, like "this room is a pigsty."

meter Repeated rhythm.

rhyme Two words that sound alike, sometimes at the end of a line, like "ham" and "jam."

rhythm A pattern of sounds.

simile A word or phrase that compares two different things using "like" or "as," for instance, "black as night."

stanza A group of lines arranged together in a poem.

structure An arrangement in a pattern.

verse A line of writing that has a certain rhythm.

CONTENTS

WORDS TO KNOW 2

POEMS YOU KNOW 5

WHAT'S A POEM? 7

KINDS OF POEMS 9

LOOKIN' GOOD 11

HEAR THE RHYTHM 13

HEAR THE RHYME 15

FIDDLING AROUND WITH RHYME 17

FOCUS ON FORM 19

A SIMPLE SIMILE 21

ACTIVITY: WRITE YOUR OWN POEM 22

LEARN MORE 24

INDEX 24

The nursery rhyme about a cow jumping over the moon is a poem.

Poems You Know

You probably already know lots of poems! Nursery rhymes like "Hey, diddle, diddle / the cat and the fiddle," are poems. Nursery rhymes are usually simple and funny.

FAST FACT

Young children can learn how to talk by listening to poems.

**Poems look and
sound different
from other
kinds of writing**

What's a Poem?

Poems are a kind of **literature**. They are written in **verse**. Poems often have **rhythm** and **rhyme**. The poet chooses each word carefully.

Old Mother Goose, when
She wanted to wander,
Would ride through the air
On a very fine gander.

Mother Goose
rhymes were
poems written for
children hundreds
of years ago.

Kinds of Poems

There are all kinds of poems. Poems can be about real life. Some are about nature. Others tell a story. Some poems are written to honor a person.

FAST FACT

Mother Goose may have been a real person named Elizabeth.

Tiger, tiger, burning bright
In the forests of the night,
What immortal hand or eye
Could frame thy fearful symmetry?

William Blake

This stanza about a tiger is four lines long. The whole poem has six stanzas.

Lookin' Good

Sometimes poems are defined by how they look. This is called **structure**. Some poems are arranged in groups of lines. These are called **stanzas**.

FAST FACT

The longest poem ever written has 1.8 million words.

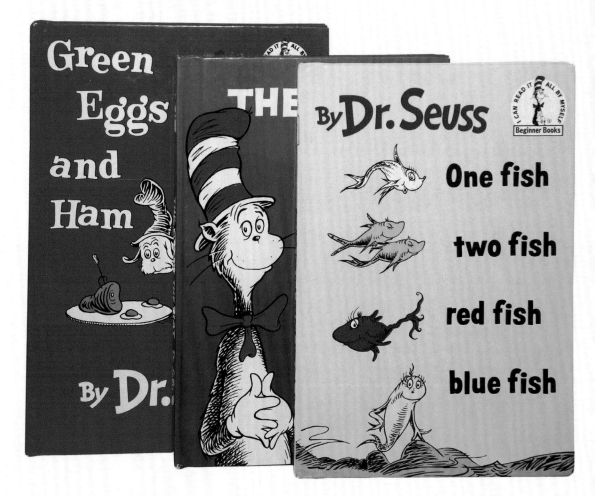

Dr. Seuss poems have a simple but strong rhythm.

Hear the Rhythm

Some poems have a pattern in the words. Poets write their words in rhythm. Rhythm makes the poem fun to read. It may also make the poem easy to remember.

FAST FACT

Music has rhythm, too!
It is called the beat.

Teachers can teach very young students about rhyme by reading poems to them.

Hear the Rhyme

Sounds are important in poetry. Poets sometimes use patterns of sound. Some poets use **rhyme**. This means that some of the words have the same sound.

It's easy to rhyme! Think of a simple word. What other words sound like it?

Fiddling Around with Rhyme

Do you remember the nursery rhyme from the first chapter? "Hey, diddle, *diddle* / The cat and the *fiddle*." The last word of each line rhymes.

FAST FACT

World Poetry Day is March 21.

This young girl won
a contest for writing
her own haiku.

freshly mown grass

clinging to my shoes

my muddled thoughts

Gracie Starkey

Focus on Form

Some poets follow special rules to write poems. These might have a certain pattern for **meter** and rhyme. A haiku is an example of a form. It has three lines.

"Elephant in the room" is a figure of speech that means a big problem nobody wants to talk about.

A Simple Simile

Many poems use **figure of speech**. One is called a **simile**. Similes compare things using the words "like" or "as." She was "as wise as an owl" is a simile.

FAST FACT

Metaphors compare things, too. "A blanket of snow" is a metaphor.

Activity

Write Your Own Poem

MATERIALS
- notebook
- pencil

It's easy to write your own poem. One way is to write a riddle

poem. Write down the following lines and fill in the blanks to describe something:

I smell like _____.

I taste like _____.

I feel like _____.

I sound like_____.

What am I?

Share your riddle poem with friends and family.

LEARN MORE

Books

Angelou, Maya. *Poems for Young People*. New York, NY: Sterling Children's Books, 2013.

Barker, Geoff. *What Is a Poem?* New York, NY: Britannica Educational Publishing, 2014.

Proudfit, Benjamin. *Writing Poems*. New York, NY: Gareth Stevens Library, 2015.

Websites

Ken Nesbitt's Poetry4Kids
www.poetry4kids.com/
Read poems, play games, learn about rhyming, write your own poems, and more!

Poems Kids Like
www.poets.org/poetsorg/text/poems-kids
Search for all kinds of poems for kids.

The Official Robert Munsch Site: Poems
robertmunsch.com/poems-stories
Check out funny poems by Robert Munsch.

INDEX

figure of speech, 21

form, 19

nursery rhymes, 5, 17

rhyme, 7, 15, 17, 19

rhythm, 7, 13

simile, 21

stanza, 11

structure, 11

Published in 2019 by Enslow Publishing, LLC.
101 W. 23rd Street, Suite 240, New York, NY 10011

Copyright © 2019 by Enslow Publishing, LLC.

Library of Congress Cataloging-in-Publication Data

Names: Niver, Heather Moore author.
Title: Poems / Heather Moore Niver.
Description: New York : Enslow Publishing, 2019. | Series: Let's learn about literature | Includes bibliographical references and index. | Audience: Grades K-4. | Identifiers: LCCN 2017047943| ISBN 9780766097551 (library bound) | ISBN 9780766097568 (pbk.) | ISBN 9780766097575 (6 pack)
Subjects: LCSH: Poetry—History and criticism—Juvenile literature.
Classification: LCC PN1136 .N55 2018 | DDC 809.1—dc23
LC record available at https://lccn.loc.gov/2017047943

Printed in the United States of America

Photo Credits: Cover, p. 1 Yiorgos GR/Shutterstock.com; pp. 2–3, 24 Gurza/Shutterstock.com; pp. 4, 8 Niday Picture Library/Alamy Stock Photo; pp. 5, 7, 9, 11, 13, 15, 17, 19, 21, 22–23 (paper, notebook, pencil) narmacero/Shutterstock.com; pp. 5, 7, 11, 15, 17, 19, 21, 22 (open book) Wen Wen/Shutterstock.com; p. 6 mizar_21984/Shutterstock.com; p. 10 GromovPro/Shutterstock.com; p. 12 Julie Clopper/Shutterstock.com; p. 14 Monkey Business Images/Shutterstock.com; p. 16 Lorelyn Medina/Shutterstock.com; p. 18 Kyodo News/Getty Images; p. 20 Brian A Jackson/Shutterstock.com; p. 22 Vanatchanan/Shutterstock.com.